D0194790

The
WORST-CASE SCENARIO
POCKET GUIDE
DOGS

By David Borgenicht &
Sam Stall

Illustrations by Brenda Brown

CHRONICLE BOOKS
SAN FRANCISCO

Copyright © 2009 by Quirk Productions, Inc.

Library of Congress Cataloging-in-Publication Data
available.

ISBN: 978-0-8118-6812-9

Manufactured in China.
Designed by Jenny Kraemer.
Illustrations by Brenda Brown.
Visit www.worstcasescenarios.com

10 9 8 7 6 5 4 3 2 1

Chronicle Books LLC
680 Second Street
San Francisco, CA 94107
www.chroniclebooks.com

CONTENTS

Introduction . . . 4

1 It's a Dog Eat Dog World . . . 9
Out and About

2 In the Doghouse . . . 29
Trouble at Home

3 Sick as a Dog . . . 65
First Aid

Index . . . 90

Acknowledgments . . . 93

About the Authors . . . 94

INTRODUCTION

They are companions, protectors, and exercise buddies. They are footwarmers, snugglers, and good listeners. They are always sad to see us go, and always overjoyed to see us return. With their boundless energy, undying loyalty, and a remarkable ability to comfort us on even the dreariest of days, dogs are like living, breathing, slobbery manifestations of unconditional love.

But they're not perfect. Dogs can be noisemakers. Dogs can turn $150 loafers into chew toys faster than you can blink. Dogs mark their territory with gleeful abandon, shed their coats, and often make inappropriate displays of affection. In short, dogs can turn from best-case compatriots to worst-case scenarios faster than you can say, "Kingston—NO! Bad dog!"

That's where this handy little volume comes in. *The Worst-Case Scenario Pocket Guide: Dogs* offers step-by-step solutions to the biggest canine conundrums, from puppy proofing your home to performing the Heimlich, from getting rid of skunk odor to dealing with a digger. We've also included handy charts, lists, and instant solutions for a variety of problems. If you need to know four different methods for poop stain removal, look no further.

We're not trying to frighten you out of dog ownership—we just want you to be ready if your sweet wittle Fido unexpectedly turns into Cujo.

So be prepared   and take solace in the fact that this book can double as an emergency scooper.

—The Authors

You do not own a dog, the dog owns you.
—Author Unknown

Chapter 1
Out and About

IT'S A DOG EAT DOG WORLD

HOW TO FEND OFF A VICIOUS DOG

1 Hide.
Take refuge in an unlocked car, tree, or other protected space. Do not attempt to seek safety unless you are certain you can make it.

2 Stand your ground.
When the dog approaches, do not run. It makes you look weak, or like prey.

3 Look tough.
Stand tall. Appear confident.

4 Sound tough.
Tell him "No," in a firm voice. Speak loudly but do not shout.

5 Do not make prolonged eye contact.

6 | Back away slowly.
Dogs are highly territorial and will often lose interest once you leave their home base. Remain aware of the canine's whereabouts as you withdraw.

7 | Defend yourself.
After the dog snarls and lunges, use sticks or hurl shoes to keep the dog out of biting range. If the dog hesitates, charge and scream as loudly as possible. A sudden show of strength may end the encounter or it may antagonize the dog. Remain on your feet and out of biting range.

8 | Divert the attack.
Remove your jacket and wrap it loosely around one of your arms. Hold the protected arm in front of you and make it an inviting and obvious target. When the dog latches onto your coat, quickly pull your arm free of the garment and flee.

Take refuge in a tree.

9 Curl up.

If you stumble or the dog makes contact, roll your body into the fetal position. Use your hands to protect your throat and face. Do not get up until you are sure the dog has departed.

Be Aware

- Fleeing an attacking canine is both dangerous (it exposes your vulnerable back, buttocks, and calves to attack) and pointless (the top speed of a typical human is 15 mph; a dog can reach 45 mph).
- There is no such thing as a "minor" dog bite. What looks like a simple puncture wound may conceal muscle damage caused when the animal latched on and violently shook his head. Also, bites can lead to infection—even, possibly, to rabies. Seek medical attention no matter how minor the injuries may seem.

FIVE DOGS YOU NEVER
WANT TO ANTAGONIZE

Perro de Presa Canario	Name means "Canarian Dog of Prey." Developed in the Canary Islands and used by the Conquistadors as a terror weapon against Native Americans. Infamous for its "man-stopping" ability.
Neapolitan Mastiff	Created to fight gladiators and wild animals in Roman times. Can weigh as much as 150 pounds.
Tosa	Massive Japanese fighting dog that can weigh between 80 and 120 pounds.
Bandog or Bandogge	Extremely powerful guardian dog produced by crossing pit bull terriers with mastiff varieties—particularly the forbidding Neapolitan Mastiff. Weighs in excess of 100 pounds.
Dogo Argentino	Looks like an all-white, very large pit bull. Developed in Argentina to take on boars and cougars. Would have absolutely no trouble with you. Can weigh 80 to 100 pounds.

HOW TO RESCUE A DROWNING DOG

1 Do not dash into the water.
A panicked, drowning dog, like a drowning human, is extremely dangerous to potential rescuers. A poor swimmer or physically weak person who enters the water to help a large dog runs the risk of being taken down with the animal.

2 Throw in a life preserver or other flotation device.
Dogs will lunge toward anything that floats. If the device is attached to a rope, pull him in. If the flotation device is not attached to a rope, the dog will most likely find a way to paddle with it.

3 Hook the dog's collar with a pole.
Use a tree branch, fence rail, or length of pipe to pull the dog to safety.

Tow the dog back to shore.

4   Row out to the dog.
If the dog is large and the boat is small, do
not allow him to capsize the vessel by trying
to scramble aboard.

5   Tow the dog back to shore with a
flotation device.

INSTANT SOLUTION

RESUSCITATE A DROWNED DOG

*Hold the dog upside down by its rear legs for 15 to 20 seconds,
giving several downward shakes to help expel fluid. If dog is
too big to lift, place head down on a sloping surface.*

HOW TO GET RID OF SKUNK ODOR ON YOUR DOG

1. Keep the dog outside.

2. Flush the dog's eyes with water.

3. Change your clothes and remove jewelry. The compound used to remove skunk odor can discolor fabric and, in contact with metals, irritate skin.

4. Prepare special odor-removing wash. Mix one quart of 3 percent hydrogen peroxide with ¼ cup of baking soda and 1 teaspoon of liquid dish soap. Ingredients will bubble furiously when combined. This quantity is sufficient for a medium-sized dog. A larger canine may need more.

*Place dog in outdoor tub and work odor-removing
mixture into fur.*

5 Apply mixture immediately.
Use the odor-removing compound while
still foaming, as this is when it is most
effective. Place dog in bathtub or outdoor
tub and work mixture into fur, avoiding
mouth and eyes. Leave for several minutes
or until the foaming stops, then rinse
thoroughly. Reapply if odor persists.

6 Dry the dog.

7 Repeat washing, if necessary.
This treatment can irritate a dog's skin,
so wait at least 48 hours before bathing
a second time.

Be Aware
- Skunk spray consists of the ejected
  contents of the animal's anal glands. A
  freshly sprayed canine can transfer the
  scent to carpet, furniture, and anything
  else he brushes against. The odor can
  cause nausea and dizziness in humans.

- Discard the dog's collar or harness. It will spread skunk odor to anything it touches, and isn't worth the extensive effort it would take to deodorize it.
- Skunks can carry rabies. Examine your pet for bites.

COMMON DOG MESSES

Burrs	Tease out with metal comb. If buried more deeply, apply vegetable oil liberally to separate coat from burr. Crush burrs with pliers, or employ scissors.
Chewing gum	Use the same method applied to gum in hair. Place ice on the gum to inhibit stickiness, then pull or clip free. Commercial gum-removal products are also available.
Paint	If latex-based, soak affected area in water for at least five minutes. Then remove pliant paint by rubbing coated hair vigorously between fingers. Clip hair covered with oil-based paint. Do not use paint removers, as these are highly toxic if the dog consumes them (by licking his fur).
Tar	Apply petroleum jelly to small portion of affected area, then wipe off broken-up tar with a clean cloth. Repeat as necessary. Afterward, wash canine with degreasing shampoo. If area of coverage is too large, consider clipping.

INSTANT SOLUTION

SURVIVE A ROAD TRIP WITH YOUR DOG

*For small and medium-sized dogs, equip a crate with
favorite toys, a blanket, and other comforting items from
home. Secure larger dogs using a harness strap.
Do not allow the dog to roam freely in the car.*

THREE BELOVED DOG BREEDS AND THINGS YOU NEVER WANT TO DO WITH THEM

Old English Bulldogs	Take them swimming. Bulldogs are very poorly designed for water work and float about as competently as bricks.
Great Danes	Give them a big meal. Danes, like other deep-chested dogs, are prone to a horrible condition called bloat, or stomach torsion. If they ingest a large quantity of food quickly, their stomach can literally spin, tying it off on each end like a sausage.
Pugs	Take them for a long walk on a hot day. This dog's pushed-in nose compromises breathing. A half-hour walk in the middle of summer would be excessive.

PERSONALITIES/LIFESTYLES AND

Personality	Breed to Avoid
Couch Potato	Border Collie
Athlete	Pekingese
Married with Young Children	Chow Chow
Neat Freak	Rough Collie
Married with Older Children	Miniature Pinscher
Senior Citizen	Sheltie
Apartment Dweller	Newfoundland

the Dogs They Should Avoid

Danger

Becomes mentally unbalanced if not regularly exercised

Hates walks and most other forms of physical exertion

Doesn't like children

Constant, appalling shedding

Nippy and intolerant of rough handling

Nervous and hyperactive; prone to excessive barking

Enormous and hairy

CHAPTER 2
TROUBLE AT HOME

IN THE DOGHOUSE

HOW TO PUPPY-PROOF YOUR HOME

⭐ Survey your home from a "puppy's eye view."
Get low to the ground and examine your home from the animal's perspective.

⭐ Secure objects that can be chewed.
Tape electrical cords high enough on the wall so the puppy cannot reach them, or protect them with hard plastic or rubber runners. Remove choking hazards such as buttons, small toys, coins, and jewelry. Place shoes, clothing, books, CDs, children's toys, and other potential teething targets out of the puppy's reach.

⭐ Secure objects than can be peed on.

Secure objects that can be chewed, peed on, scratched, broken, swallowed, or otherwise destroyed.

★ Secure objects that can be scratched.

★ Secure objects that can be broken.

★ Secure objects that can be swallowed.

★ Secure plants.
Restrict access to houseplants and flower arrangements, many of which—including daffodils, hydrangeas, and philodendrons—are dangerous to canines if ingested.

★ Secure poisons.
Restrict access to household cleaners, anti-freeze, and insect/animal repellants. Lock up products containing nicotine, caffeine, and alcohol.

★ Protect the furniture.
Paint the furniture covering with a bad-tasting product called "bitter apple."

✪ **Restrict access to the rest of your home.** Use child gates to close off rooms containing easily damaged furnishings, or to secure potentially hazardous locations such as bathrooms or basement steps. Prevent access to trash cans, toilets, and fireplaces, which are dangerous when in use and dirty when they are not.

Be Aware

- If you would not allow a toddler access to an object, the puppy should not have access to it either.
- Puppyhood is the best time to get a dog accustomed to your cat.

HOUSEHOLD ITEMS THAT ARE

U.S. pennies

Chocolate

Onions

Garlic

Antifreeze

Macadamia nuts

Raisins and grapes

Tobacco

Alcohol

Mistletoe

Toxic to Canines

One-cent coins minted since 1982, which contain high concentrations of zinc, can cause anemia, kidney and liver failure

The darker the variety, the more dangerous; theobromine, a natural stimulant found in chocolate, can cause arrhythmia, seizures, muscle tremors, and coma

Can cause destruction of red blood cells, triggering severe anemia

Can also trigger severe anemia

Dogs are attracted by its sweet taste; very toxic

Can cause depression, weakness, muscular stiffness, vomiting, tremors, elevated heart rate

Can cause renal failure in dogs who eat large amounts

Can cause severe vomiting, elevated heart rate, blood pressure drops, seizures, respiratory failure

Even small amounts can cause alcohol poisoning; the smaller the dog, the greater the danger

Triggers gastrointestinal disorders and cardiovascular collapse

INSTANT SOLUTION

GET YOUR DOG TO EXERCISE MORE

*Incorporate more exercise, such as jogging,
into your dog's daily routine.*

HOW TO SILENCE A BARKING ADDICT

⭐ Give your dog more attention.
Many canines bark out of loneliness.
Increased quality time with your pet can
help mitigate her tendency to vocalize.

⭐ Give your dog less attention.
Do not comfort a barking dog. Do not
reinforce the idea that making noise reaps
benefits.

⭐ Use negative reinforcement techniques.
Startle the dog in mid-bark by rattling
a soft drink can containing a handful
of coins. At the same time, say "Quiet!"
in a firm voice. Eventually the dog will
respond to the command alone.

✪ **Do not shout at the dog.**
Remain calm. If the dog barks because she believes she is defending her territory, seeing her owner become agitated will only reinforce her view that defense is warranted.

✪ **Introduce your dog to people she finds threatening.**
Dogs will bark at frequent visitors such as mail carriers. Arrange a face-to-face "meet and greet" with such regular strangers. If the canine sees the person as a known quantity, she may respond less aggressively. Closely supervise such meetings.

✪ **Reward silence in your absence.**
Walk out the front door as if you are going somewhere. Say "Quiet" to your dog as you leave. When the dog begins to bark, step back in and say "Quiet" again. Leave once more. Only return when the dog is silent— even if she is only silent for a few seconds.

Introduce your dog to people she finds threatening.

Praise the animal profusely for not barking. Repeat the exercise daily until the barking ceases.

⭐ **Close the drapes.**
Prevent the dog from barking incessantly at passersby by denying her a clear view of the outdoors.

How to Stop Your Neighbor's Dog from Barking

⭐ **Do not ring your neighbor's bell.**
Ringing the doorbell may antagonize the dog to bark more if he believes he is defending his territory.

⭐ **Do not yell at the dog.**

⭐ **Do not toss raw meat at the dog.**

⭐ **Do not call the police.**

✪ **Do not call your neighbor names.**
Be tactful. Refrain from shouting epithets or accusing your neighbor of thoughtlessness or irresponsibility.

✪ **Do not try to drown out the noise with loud music.**
Loud music will only exacerbate the situation and exasperate your other neighbors.

TOP REASONS FOR
CANINE VET VISITS

1. Ear infections

2. Skin allergies

3. Pyoderma (hot spots)

4. Stomach upsets

5. Intestinal inflammation/diarrhea

6. Bladder diseases

7. Eye infections

8. Arthritis

9. Hypothyroidism

10. Sprains

HOW TO DEAL
WITH A DIGGER

⭐ Do not ignore the dog.
Play with him before you leave him alone.
Leave the dog a few toys he can play with
outdoors. If left outside for too long, many
canines will dig out of boredom.

⭐ Keep the dog inside.
On hot days, overheated dogs often seek
to uncover a cool patch of earth upon
which to lie.

⭐ Cover up the dog's favorite digging spot.
Mark the area "off limits" by using a heavy
tarp, a sheet of plywood, or some other
nonpermeable barrier.

⭐ Place some of the dog's own feces in his
favorite digging spot.
The next time the dog digs, he will

Trouble at Home

*Lead your dog to a designated digging area and make
a great show of digging.*

uncover an unpleasant surprise. This is often enough of an incentive to change his behavior.

⭐ Create a special digging space for the dog. Excavate a small portion of the yard to a depth of about a foot, then fill the depression with sand. Bury treats and some of the dog's toys in the sand, then lead him to the area and make a great show of digging. Directing the canine's efforts toward this spot will likely make it his favorite—and exclusive—excavation zone.

Be Aware

While many dogs dig out of boredom, some breeds are genetically predisposed to this behavior. Many varieties of terriers, whose name means "earth dog," were bred to rout animals out of their underground lairs. Disabusing them of this inborn drive can be extremely difficult, if not impossible.

COMMANDS A DOG WILL NEVER UNDERSTAND

Long commands	A command must be succinct. "Pepper, off!" will work, "Pepper, please get off the couch right now!" will not work.
Multiple commands	"Stop barking and lie down" is too much information.
Abstract commands	"Be considerate" is too abstract of a concept for the dog to understand.
Telepathic commands	Dogs are sometimes thought to have telepathic powers. They do not. However, they are really good at reading human behavior.

HOW TO PREVENT YOUR DOG FROM MARKING HIS TERRITORY INDOORS

⭐ Watch the dog closely.
Carefully monitor your dog's behavior. When you sense he is about to mark, register your disapproval by vigorously shaking a can containing some loose change. Then, escort him outside to urinate.

⭐ Confine the dog in a crate when you leave the house.
Most dogs will not, except in extraordinary circumstances, soil their own sleeping place.

⭐ Clean.
Thoroughly wash and deodorize all

previously marked locations. The scent of their own urine encourages dogs to revisit these spots. Clean marked areas with commercially available, enzyme-based products, or a homemade mix of 50 percent white vinegar, 50 percent water. Normal household cleaners are not thorough enough.

✪ **Neuter your dog.**
Male dogs urinate as a sexual display or as a challenge to rivals. Neutering, preferably at an early age, can stop this behavior.

Be Aware
- Dog urine fluoresces when illuminated by a black light. Use one to find old stains.
- Do not admonish a dog for marking unless you catch him in the act. A minute or two later, the animal will not understand why he is being punished. Never strike or otherwise physically punish your dog.

Wash and deodorize all previously marked locations.
Use black light to find old stains.

TECHNIQUES FOR CLEANING POOP STAINS FROM CARPET

Commercial laundry detergent	Apply it to the carpet, either mildly diluted or straight, depending on the stain's severity. Scrub vigorously, then rinse with water. Repeat as many times as necessary.
Ammonia and water	Blot the stain using a mix of 2 tablespoons ammonia in 1 cup of water. Rinse with cold water. Repeat if necessary.
Commercial, enzyme-based product	Use a commercial dog poop-cleaning product that employs enzymes to break down organic matter. Hydrogen peroxide–based cleaning products may also be effective.
High-pressure, commercial rug shampoo units	Use to rid your carpets of any fecal remnants.

HOW TO TEACH AN OLD DOG NEW TRICKS

★ Be patient.
You are asking a dog not just to learn something new, but to unlearn her previous way of doing things. This takes time.

★ Credit the dog.
Convince the dog that she came up with the new trick on her own. If teaching an older canine to "sit," do not try to force her into a sitting position. Instead, praise and reward her when she sits on her own, all the while repeating the "sit" command. Eventually the dog will perform the appropriate behavior when she hears the appropriate word.

*Consider joining a class. The example of other dogs
may help her catch on.*

★ Keep training sessions short.
Older dogs tire more easily, so spend only about 10 to 15 minutes on any one training session. Do one in the morning and one in the afternoon, always at the same times.

★ Keep sessions fun.
Many older, savvy canines "play dumb" during training sessions in order to get out of learning something new.

★ Reinforce good behavior.
Use praise and treats to strongly reward compliance.

Be Aware
- Do not go overboard on food rewards. An older, less-active dog may start to put on weight.
- If your dog is particularly stubborn, consider joining a training class. The example of other dogs may help her catch on.

INSTANT SOLUTION

BRUSH YOUR DOG'S TEETH

Use peanut butter as toothpaste.

THE MOST DIFFICULT-
TO-TRAIN BREEDS

1. Afghan Hound

2. Basenji

3. English Bulldog

4. Chow Chow

5. Borzoi

6. Bloodhound

7. Pekingese

8. Mastiff and Beagle

9. Basset Hound

10. Shih Tzu

HOW TO HAIR-PROOF YOUR HOME

★ Watch the calendar.
Dogs with ample amounts of hair often "blow their coats" during fall and spring. The shedding during these periods can be truly epic, so keep the dogs outside more during those seasons.

★ Treat your dog to special bathing and hair-care regimens.
Consider special bathing and hair-care regimens that use a mild, nonirritating shampoo. Shampoos that are fortified with omega-3 and omega-6 fatty acids can reduce shedding and help to maintain healthy skin. Do not overbathe as that can have a drying effect by removing natural oils.

Convince your kids that grooming the dog is fun.

✪ Use a bag-less vacuum cleaner.

✪ Clean your ducts.
Rid your ductwork of excessive pet hair, which can accumulate in great mounds, aggravating the allergies of anyone sensitive to dander.

✪ Convince your kids that grooming the dog is a "fun thing."
Teach them how to use a grooming brush, and have them brush the dog daily outside.

Be Aware
Some breeds, such as the poodle, either shed very little or not at all. However, most still require grooming to keep their hair in order.

DOGS THAT REQUIRE LITTLE, AVERAGE, AND INTENSIVE GROOMING

Almost no grooming: Hair usually is short, with no undercoat	American Staffordshire Terrier, Boxer, English Bulldog, Whippet
Little grooming: Short or moderate-length hair, minimal or no undercoat	Basset Hound, Dachshund, French Bulldog, Greyhound, Rhodesian Ridgeback
Average grooming: Moderate-length hair, plus undercoat	Border Collie, Cairn Terrier, Irish Setter, Newfoundland, Pomeranian, West Highland Terrier
Intensive grooming: Long hair, usually over a thick undercoat	Afghan Hound, Bichon Frise, Borzoi, Chow Chow, Collie, Old English Sheepdog, Pekingese, Sheltie

HOW TO GET YOUR DOG TO LIKE YOUR SIGNIFICANT OTHER

✪ Introduce the canine to your significant other on neutral ground.
Coordinate the first meeting at a public place, such as a nearby park. Avoid introducing the two on the dog's home turf, which risks encouraging the dog to defend his territory around a stranger.

✪ Instruct your significant other to approach the dog calmly.
This is particularly important if your pet is overly fearful or very dominant. Advise your companion to avoid prolonged eye contact (which can be construed as a threat) or immediately and enthusiastically petting the canine (which the dog might

Wear an article of your partner's clothing to familiarize the canine with her scent.

find unnerving). Coach your partner to greet the animal in a low-key manner. Later, if the dog seems amenable, your significant other can offer a pat on the back. Do not overdo it.

⭐ **Provide treats.**
Praise your dog for good behavior and offer him a treat. Even better, have your significant other offer him a treat.

⭐ **Wear a garment that has been in contact with your new companion.**
When alone with your dog, wear an article of your partner's clothing. This will help familiarize the canine with your significant other's scent, making your dog more at ease when he actually encounters your significant other.

⭐ **Have your significant other feed the dog.**
Occasionally a canine may develop dominance issues with a newcomer. To diffuse

this, have your new friend feed the dog for a while. Being in charge of the animal's sustenance will make the person seem "dominant" in the eyes of your pet.

Be Aware

- A "significant other" might be a lover, a new roommate, or a newborn baby. Most of these steps also apply to introducing another dog, cat, or llama.
- If your dog's suspicion and distrust of a new acquaintance seems unshakable, do not dismiss it. Canines are experts at "reading" human personalities and intentions. He may understand your new friend's true nature far better than you do.

Chapter 3
First Aid

SICK AS A DOG

HOW TO GIVE A DOG ARTIFICIAL RESPIRATION

1 Listen for a heartbeat.
Place your ear against the left side of the canine's chest.

2 Check for breathing.
Place a mirror in front of the dog's nose and look for condensation. Alternatively, place a cotton ball before the nose and watch for movement in the cotton filaments.

3 Clear the airway.
Lay the dog on her side, tilt the head back, and move the tongue aside. Locate and remove anything blocking breathing.

4 Straighten the dog's neck.

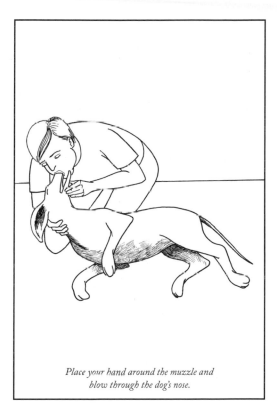

*Place your hand around the muzzle and
blow through the dog's nose.*

5 Breathe through the dog's nose.
For medium to large dogs, place your hand around the muzzle. Hold it closed and place your mouth over the nose. For smaller dogs, position your mouth to cover her nose and lips.

6 Repeat four or five quick, forceful breaths.

7 Check for response.
If normal breathing commences, stop. If not, or if breathing is very shallow, continue rescue breathing. Give 20 breaths per minute for small dogs, 20 to 30 breaths per minute for medium and large dogs.

8 Check for a heartbeat.
Place your hand on the left side of the dog's chest.

9 Continue rescue breathing and position dog for chest compressions.

How to Give Your Dog CPR

1 Position the dog on her side.
The back is better for barrel-chested breeds.
Make sure the dog is on a firm surface.

2 Kneel next to the dog.

3 Compress the chest.
For small dogs, place your palm and finger-
tips over the ribs at the point where the
elbow meets the chest. Compress the chest
approximately one inch, twice per second.
Alternate every five compressions with one
breath. For medium to large dogs, extend
your elbows and cup your hands on top of
each other. Place hands over the ribs at the
point where the dog's elbows meet the
chest, then compress it two to three inches,
one-and-a-half to two times per second.
Alternate every five compressions with
one breath. For dogs that weigh more than
100 pounds, compress the chest two or

three inches once per second, alternating every ten compressions with a breath.

4 Check for a heartbeat.
After one minute, listen for a heartbeat. If none is found, continue with compressions.

Be Aware
A dog's pulse cannot be felt at the neck.

HOME CANINE MEDICAL KIT

- Cotton roll and cotton balls
- Gauze pads and gauze tape
- Scissors
- Saline eyewash
- Oral syringes
- Large towel
- Exam gloves
- 1-inch surgical tape
- Ice pack
- Digital thermometer
- Hydrocortisone cream
- Diphenhydramine (Benadryl)
- Tweezers
- Muzzle
- Leash
- Plastic toolbox to serve as emergency kit
- Sticker with pet hospital and veterinarian's phone numbers

HOW TO GIVE A DOG A PILL

1 | Sit on the floor in front of your dog.
Place smaller dogs on your lap.

2 | Grasp the dog's head using your non-dominant hand.
Be firm but not harsh. Place your hand on top of the muzzle, with your thumb on one side and fingers on the other.

3 | Raise up the dog's nose.
Squeeze firmly behind the canine or "eye" teeth until the jaw opens.

4 | Place the pill between the thumb and forefinger of your dominant hand.
Use the hand's other three fingers to open the lower jaw farther.

5 | Place the pill far back in the dog's mouth.

Use your hand to keep the dog's mouth closed
after placing the pill in his mouth.

6 Close the mouth.

7 Tilt up the chin.
Keep the mouth closed and stroke the throat to help with swallowing.

8 Give the dog a treat.

Be Aware

- Blowing on the nose may stimulate the dog to swallow.
- Hiding the pill in peanut butter or some other treat the dog covets is the easiest way to administer a pill. However, some canines become quite adept at eating the treat and leaving the pill.

INSTANT SOLUTION

TAKE A DOG'S TEMPERATURE

Lubricate the thermometer with petroleum jelly.
Insert the thermometer about 1 inch into the rectum.
Hold until thermometer beeps. Remove slowly.

HOW TO GIVE A DOG THE HEIMLICH MANEUVER

1 Check for throat obstructions.
Open the dog's mouth and inspect the back of the throat, looking for the object causing the obstruction. If you see it, carefully remove it. If the dog is unconscious, pull the tongue forward for a better view.

2 Shake the obstruction free.
If the dog is small, pick him up and hold him by the hips with his head hanging down. For larger dogs, hold the hind legs so that the head hangs down. If this fails to dislodge the obstruction, place the dog back on the ground and proceed to the next step.

3 Place your arms around the dog's waist.
With the dog standing or lying down, clasp

Place your arms around the dog's waist below the last rib and compress the stomach.

your hands together around the stomach, placing them just behind the last rib.

4   Compress the stomach.
Push up five times rapidly.

5   Check for an obstruction.
Sweep the dog's mouth with your fingers to see if the object was dislodged.

6   Repeat.
If the object has not come free, strike the dog firmly between the shoulder blades with the flat side of one hand, and then do another five abdominal compressions. Alternate the back-slapping and compressions until the object is knocked free.

Be Aware

An unconscious dog may still bite reflexively. Be careful when sweeping the mouth. When jarring the obstruction free by striking the dog, do not hit him so hard as to injure him.

SIGNS YOUR DOG MAY NEED PSYCHOTHERAPY

Phobias	Fear of hats, car horns, or feet can indicate the dog was once harmed by someone or something connected to these objects
Obsessive Compulsive Disorder	Nonsensical, excessive repetitive behavior may be signs of boredom, separation anxiety, or severe stress
Excessive Aggression or Timidity	The problem may be genetic disposition to these traits, or rough handling during puppyhood
Extreme Grief	Refusal to groom, exercise, or eat in response to the loss of an animal companion or human may be a sign of depression

HOW TO TRANSPORT A WOUNDED DOG WHEN HIKING

1 Stabilize any wounds or injuries.
If there is an open, bleeding wound, apply
a cloth and pressure to stop blood loss.

2 Apply a muzzle.
Pass a piece of cloth, rope, or similar
item around the mouth several times, tie
underneath (not too tight), then tie the
line again behind the neck.

3 Carry the dog.
A small dog (under 30 pounds) can be
carried in your arms. However, this can
become a severe physical trial to a hiker
also burdened with a heavy pack and
traveling over uneven, unfamiliar territory.

Chapter 3: Sick as a Dog

Fashion a travois out of sticks and clothing.

A larger dog can be carried over the shoulders—though this may necessitate abandoning one's pack. Do not do this unless you are familiar with the area and are sure you can reach safety in a relatively short amount of time.

4 Make a stretcher.
If you have a hiking partner, locate or cut two poles, then drape coats, extra clothing, or tent material between them. Secure with rope, leather straps, or any other available material. Place the dog on the stretcher and lift, grasping the ends of the two poles and hoisting up. Keep the stretcher as level as possible when walking.

5 Make a travois.
If you are alone, cut two poles and lash them together at one end. At the other end, lash on a "spacer bar" approximately two to three feet wide. Drape coats, extra clothing, or tent material between the two

longer poles, then secure them with any available material. Place the dog on the travois and begin pulling at the "narrow" end. Ease this chore by hooking a rope around the end of the travois and draping it over your shoulders or around your waist.

Be Aware

- A dog may be unnerved by a stretcher or travois and refuse to lie still for transport. It may take a while to accustom the animal to the situation and win her cooperation.
- An injured dog may need to be immobilized to prevent her from doing further damage. If the canine is still ambulatory, leash her to a tree. Provide enough line for her to lie down comfortably.
- Transporting a large, incapacitated dog out of the back country can be extremely onerous, taxing even a strong, physically fit person to the limit.

INSTANT SOLUTION

MAKE AN EMERGENCY MUZZLE

*Wrap rope, fabric, or pantyhose around the dog's muzzle
several times, then pass the ends of the rope or fabric
behind the head and tie.*

Canine Traumas and How to Handle Them

Broken Bone(s)	Do not attempt to apply a splint. Cover the wound with a bandage or clean cloth.
Dog Bite	Clean wound with warm water and hydrogen peroxide.
Frostbite	Get the dog out of the cold. Rewarm the affected tissues in warm water (approximately 104°F). Do not rub or massage the tissue.
Heatstroke	Get the dog out of the heat. Immerse in a cool bath, drench in cool water, or apply cool, wet towels.
Severe Laceration	Never use a tourniquet. Place a clean towel or cloth over the wound and apply steady pressure. If blood soaks through the cloth, do not remove it; place a clean towel on top and continue applying pressure.
Snakebite	Limit the animal's movements. Do not apply a tourniquet or try to suck out the poison. Get professional help immediately.

HOW TO DEAL WITH DOG DIARRHEA

✪ Do not feed the dog for 12 to 24 hours.
Deprive the ailment of fresh "ammunition" by withholding food. However, continue to provide water, which prevents dehydration.

✪ Feed the dog a bland diet.
After at least 12 hours have passed, offer the dog boiled, skinless chicken mixed evenly with rice.

✪ Slowly return to regular diet.
If the diarrhea abates and stools form normally, gradually substitute the dog's regular menu for the chicken and rice mixture.

Do not feed the dog for 12 to 24 hours. Be sure that water is available for hydrating.

✪ Use over-the-counter "human" anti-diarrhea medications.

Under a veterinarian's advice, administer over-the-counter medicines that are safe and effective for canines. Dosages required by dogs can vary markedly from what humans need.

Be Aware

Diarrhea is a nuisance, but it can also herald dangerous problems. If the condition lasts for more than 24 hours or is accompanied by blood in the stool, pain, or general weakness, see a veterinarian immediately.

UNPLEASANT THINGS THAT CAN LIVE ON OR IN YOUR DOG

Heartworms	Mosquito-borne parasites that grow into foot-long worms that can lodge in the right ventricle of the canine heart
Hookworms	Small blood-sucking parasites that attach themselves to the walls of the small intestine, causing diarrhea, weakness, and anemia
Mites	Tiny arachnids that cause itching, hair loss, and sometimes mange, a dangerous skin condition; most extreme form is sarcoptic mange or "scabies"
Ticks	Blood-sucking parasites that can transfer Lyme disease to your dog and to humans
Fleas	Common pest that can be dangerous to puppies and weaken adult dogs; can also cause a severe allergic reaction

INDEX

A
aggression, excessive, 79
artificial respiration, 66–68

B
Bandog/Bandogge, 14
barking, stopping, 37–41
bites, 12, 85
bones, broken, 85
Border Collie, 26–27
breeds
  grooming needs, 59
  personalities/life styles and, 25–27
  training, 55
  vicious, 14
brushing teeth, 54
burr removal, 23

C
carpet, removing poop stains from, 50
chewing gum removal, 23
Chow Chow, 26–27

D
diarrhea, 86–87
digging, stopping, 43–45
dog bites, 12, 85
Dogo Argentino, 14
drowning dogs, rescuing, 15–18

E
exercise, 36

F
frostbite, 85

G
Great Dane, 25
grief, extreme, 79
grooming needs, 59

H
hair-proofing your home, 56–59
heatstroke, 85
Heimlich maneuver, 76–78
home
  hair-proofing, 56–59
  medical kits, 71

puppy-proofing,
30–35

L

laceration, severe, 85

M

marking territory
indoors, preventing,
47–49
medical kits, home, 71
messes, common, 23
Miniature Pinscher,
26–27
muzzles, emergency,
80, 84

N

Neapolitan Mastiff, 14
Newfoundland, 26–27

O

obsessive compulsive
disorder, 79
Old English Bulldog,
25

P

paint removal, 23
Pekingese, 26–27
Perro de Presa
Canario, 14

personalities/lifestyles
and breeds, 25–27
phobias, 79
pills, giving, 72–74
poisonous household
items, 34–35
poop stain cleaning, 50
psychotherapy, 79
Pug, 25
puppy-proofing your
home, 30–35

R

respiration, artificial,
66–68
resuscitation
artificial respiration,
66–68
CPR, 69–70
drowned dogs, 18
road trips, 24
Rough Collie, 26–27

S

Sheltie, 26–27
significant other,
training dog to like,
60–63
skunk odor removal,
19–22

snakebites, 85

T tar removal, 23
teeth, brushing, 54
temperature, taking, 75
territory, preventing
  marking indoors,
  47–49
timidity, excessive, 79
Tosa, 14
toxic household items,
  34–35
training
  difficult breeds, 55
  to like significant
    other, 60–63
  tricks, 51–53
transporting wounded
  dogs, 80–85
traumas, handling, 85
tricks, teaching, 51–53

V vet visit reasons, 42
vicious dogs, fending
  off, 10–14

W wounded dogs,
  transporting, 80–85

ACKNOWLEDGMENTS

David Borgenicht would like to thank Sarah O'Brien, Jay Schaefer, Steve Mockus, Brianna Smith, Jenny Kraemer, and Brenda Brown for making this book happen—you're such good buddy wuddies, yes you are, yes you are, yes, yes, yes you are!

Freelance writer and stay-at-home dad **Sam Stall** gratefully acknowledges the assistance of the various experts who, through their words and their works, helped make this book possible. He also thanks his wife for tolerating the long hours spent producing it. Most importantly he thanks his infant son, James, for refraining from crying during critical phone interviews that Daddy conducted from his desk in the basement, usually while wearing sweat pants and a milk-stained Hawaiian shirt.

ABOUT THE AUTHORS

David Borgenicht is the creator and co-author of all the books in the Worst-Case Scenario series, and is president and publisher of Quirk Books (www.quirkbooks.com). He had several dogs as a child, and he hopes they all lived very happy lives on the farms that his parents sent them to. He lives in Philadelphia.

Sam Stall is a freelance writer living in Indianapolis with his wife, Jami, son James, and their two dogs, Gracie and Trudy. Trudy is a 60-pound pit bull/German shepherd mix adopted as a puppy from a woman who stated emphatically that "she's probably a Chihuahua with some terrier mixed in, and will not get very big." He has written several other books about canines, including *The Dog Owner's Manual* and *The Good, the Bad, and the Furry: Choosing the Dog That's Right For You.*

Brenda Brown is an illustrator and cartoonist whose work has been published in many books and publications, including the Worst-Case Scenario series, *Esquire*, *Reader's Digest*, *USA Weekend*, *21st Century Science & Technology*, the *Saturday Evening Post*, and the *National Enquirer*. Her Web site is www.webtoon.com.

MORE WORST-CASE SCENARIO PRODUCTS

VISIT OUR PARTNERS' WEBSITES FOR MORE WORST-CASE SCENARIO PRODUCTS:

- ✪ Board games
  www.universitygames.com
- ✪ Gadgets
  www.protocoldesign.com
- ✪ Mobile
  www.namcogames.com/WorstCaseScenario
- ✪ Posters and puzzles
  www.aquariusimages.com/wcs.html

For updates, new scenarios, and more, visit:
www.worstcasescenarios.com

To order books visit:
www.chroniclebooks.com/worstcase

MORE WORST-CASE SCENARIOS

HANDBOOKS

- The Worst-Case Scenario Survival Handbook
- Travel
- Dating & Sex
- Golf
- Holidays
- Work
- College
- Weddings
- Parenting
- Extreme Edition
- Life

ALMANACS

- History
- Great Outdoors
- Politics

CALENDARS

- Daily Survival Calendar
- Daily Survival Calendar: Golf

POCKET GUIDES

- Dogs
- Breakups
- Retirement
- New York City